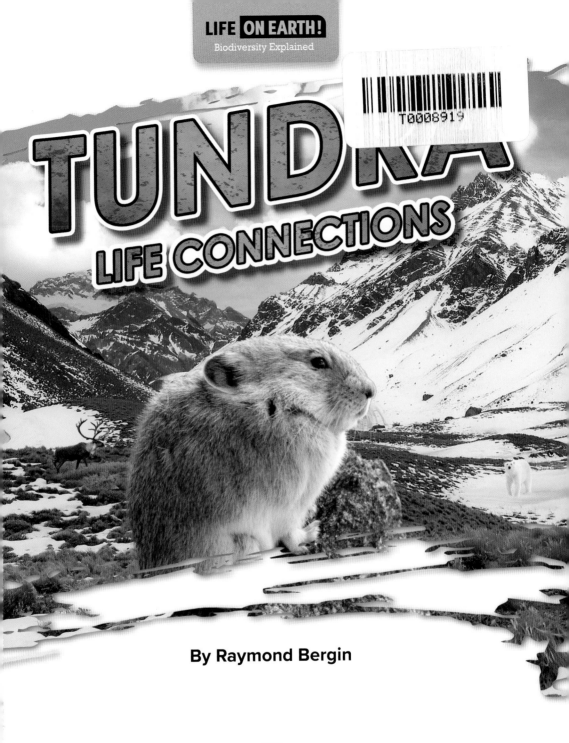

LIFE ON EARTH!
Biodiversity Explained

TUNDRA
LIFE CONNECTIONS

By Raymond Bergin

BEARPORT
PUBLISHING

Minneapolis, Minnesota

Credits

Cover and title page, © Arianna Biella / EyeEm/Getty Images, © hadynyah/iStock, © KenCanning/iStock, © Beth Ruggiero-York/Shutterstock, © pchoui/iStock, and © milehightraveler/iStock; 4–5, © Cheryl Ramalho/Alamy; 6, © mgfoto/iStock; 6–7, © Daniel A. Leifheit/Getty Images; 8–9, © pum_eva/Getty Images; 10–11, © Hans Strand/Getty Images; 12–13, © Daniel Parent/Getty Images; 14–15, © Cecilie Bergan Stuedal/Alamy; 16, © Cwieders/iStock; 16–17, © Chris Wallace/Alamy; 18–19, © twildlife/iStock; 20–21, © Andrey Nyrkov/Alamy; 22–23, © RyersonClark/iStock; 24–25, © Zoonar GmbH/Alamy; 26–27, © Danita Delimont Creative/Alamy; 28, © Gregory A. Pozhvanov/Shutterstock; 29 step 1, © wanderluster/iStock; 29 step 2, © kellyvandellen/iStock; 29 step 3, © RyanJLane/iStock; 29 step 4, © fongbeerredhot/Shutterstock; and 29 step 5, © monkeybusinessimages/iStock.

Bearport Publishing Company Product Development Team
President: Jen Jenson; Director of Product Development: Spencer Brinker; Senior Editor: Allison Juda; Editor: Charly Haley; Associate Editor: Naomi Reich; Senior Designer: Colin O'Dea; Associate Designer: Elena Klinkner; Associate Designer: Kayla Eggert; Product Development Assistant: Anita Stasson

Library of Congress Cataloging-in-Publication Data is available at www.loc.gov or upon request from the publisher.

ISBN: 979-8-88509-412-2 (hardcover)
ISBN: 979-8-88509-534-1 (paperback)
ISBN: 979-8-88509-649-2 (ebook)

For more information, write to Bearport Publishing, 5357 Penn Avenue South, Minneapolis, MN 55419.

Contents

Out in the Cold

In a frozen, rocky field, a mouselike creature hides from a white fox. A caribou munches the moss, **lichen**, and small shrubs growing nearby. Snow geese lay eggs in their nests while a hungry polar bear growls a little ways off. The arctic tundra is full of life.

But temperatures are rising and that life is changing. In the distance, unusually tall trees block sunlight and suck up water from the low plants caribou need. Animals that wouldn't normally survive the cold tundra make their way in with the warmth, spelling trouble for the animals already there. What is happening to life on Earth?

The Arctic tundra supports 1,700 different plants with 400 varieties of flowers. Hundreds of **species** of birds and land mammals also call it home.

A Planet Full of Life

Earth is made up of many **biomes**—areas of land and sea where the **climate** and natural features are perfect for certain kinds of plants and animals to live. Deserts, grasslands, forests, wetlands, oceans, and tundras are all biomes.

Every biome is home to a connected community of life. This wide variety of life is called **biodiversity**. A tundra biome can include everything from lichen and mosquitos to caribou and polar bears.

Lichen is actually two different organisms, **algae** and **fungi**, working together. Algae lives inside the fungus and gives it sugar and oxygen. In turn, the fungus gives algae the water and salt it needs to survive.

It All Fits Together

The plants and animals within biomes form communities necessary for survival. They depend upon one another for the shelter, food, and water they need. **Bacteria** in the top layer of tundra soil break down dead **vegetation** to create **nutrients** that help small, low-lying plants grow. These plants feed **grazing** animals such as elk, bison, and wild sheep.

Meanwhile, caribou dig in the soil when munching plants, sending small rodents scurrying from their hiding places. Arctic foxes follow the caribou to snatch up these furry snacks.

Each spring, swans travel to the tundra to have babies and feed on pondweed. They spread the plant's seeds when they poop, allowing new pondweed to grow the following summer.

8

Lemmings are rodents commonly found in the tundra.

The Cold, Hard Facts

Life in the tundra doesn't have it easy. Tundras are the coldest and driest of all biomes. With less than 10 inches (25 cm) of precipitation a year, they are drier than most deserts! Arctic tundras are located near the poles—in Antartica and above the Arctic Circle. Alpine tundras are found on the frozen tops of the world's tallest mountains.

In both arctic and alpine tundras, winters are long, with below-freezing temperatures for more than half the year. The summer growing season is often short. Only about two months of the year are warm enough and have enough sunlight for plants to grow in arctic tundras.

Since so little can grow in the frozen tundra, there are very few plants to die there. In other biomes, dead plants break down and add nutrients to the soil that other, larger plants and trees need to grow. Without the nutrients, tundras stay tree-free.

Thawing Earth

Much of the tundra soil—and sometimes more than a mile of earth beneath it—is frozen for most of the year. This frozen ground is called permafrost. However, a thin layer of surface soil just above the permafrost thaws in the summer. When it does, tundra plants grow shallow roots to drink up this moisture.

Caribou can't survive harsh tundra winters without lichen to eat. They can only **digest** lichen because of the bacteria living in their guts that break it down and draw out its nutrients.

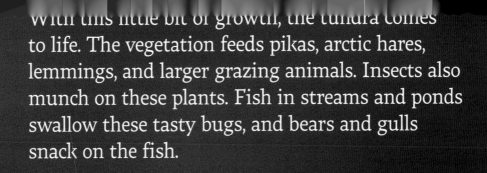

With this little bit of growth, the tundra comes to life. The vegetation feeds pikas, arctic hares, lemmings, and larger grazing animals. Insects also munch on these plants. Fish in streams and ponds swallow these tasty bugs, and bears and gulls snack on the fish.

Pikas are known to steal food from other animals to make sure they have enough for themselves.

Out of Balance

Although tundra life needs a summer thaw, too much heat can be harmful. When we burn fuel, we add a gas called **carbon dioxide** to the **atmosphere**. It traps Earth's heat, stopping it from being released into space. As a result, our planet is heating up.

Arctic foxes play an important role in the tundra community. Their pee and poop creates rich soil for plants. The foxes are also a favorite meal of polar bears, snowy owls, and wolves.

Tundra winters are getting warmer with less snowfall. Summers are hotter and drier. Some tundra plants are dying, and others are being squeezed out by warmer-weather vegetation. Grazers are having trouble finding food, and if these animals grow hungry, so will their **predators**.

Late for Dinner?

Warmer tundra winters cause the soil's top layer to thaw earlier than usual. Plant roots start to take up the nutrients, and new plants begin growing. Some tundra plants are starting to grow as much as a month early.

In spring, caribou return to the thawing Arctic from their winter homes farther south. Now, when they arrive, they find they are a little late. Plants have grown past their peak and are less nutrient-rich. Without enough good food, it is harder for caribou to have calves.

The earlier the plants grow, the fewer caribou calves are born.

Snow geese are also arriving at the tundra after plant growth has peaked. Their goslings must eat older plants, which have less of the nutrients they need.

Uninvited Guests

Warmer weather is causing other problems, too. It is thawing deeper layers of soil. This allows bigger shrubs and some trees to grow. Taller vegetation blocks sunlight and takes water from the shorter tundra plants that are important to the area's grazers. Some of these plants are even dying out.

There are areas of tundra warming so much that neighboring forests and grasslands are advancing into the space, along with the animals they support. Red foxes now attack arctic foxes in their dens and steal their food. They also kill many birds and snap up their eggs.

Years ago, grizzlies would not have been able to survive in tundras. Now, a changing climate makes it possible for them to enter these biomes.

As the tundras warm, grizzly bears are arriving to eat plants, hunt grazers, and catch fish. They now compete with polar bears for limited food and territory.

Fire and Ice

Summertime in the tundra is usually cool and damp. That's how tundra life likes it! But hotter days are drying out the soil and plant life. The ponds and rivers that usually form after the spring thaw are not appearing. Then, fish die off, and the birds and bears that eat them go hungry.

Some tundras are becoming so hot and dry that wildfires break out, killing vegetation and animals. Heat from the fires also thaws deeper layers of permafrost, allowing even more tall shrubs and trees to take root in the newly-softened ground. But they do not last during the long dry season. Then, the dried-out large plants fuel future wildfires

A tundra wildfire from above

If lichen are burned in wildfires, they can take up to 60 years to fully grow back. Caribou must leave and search elsewhere for their favorite food.

Smoke Is No Joke

Wildfire smoke has become a major source of tundra air pollution. In addition, ash from fires settles on the tundra's snow and makes it darker. The darker surface **absorbs** heat, causing the tundra to warm up even faster.

Drilling for oil and gas in the tundra causes other problems. Heavy vehicles and pipelines damage soil and uproot plants that keep permafrost cool. Pollution enters ponds and lakes, poisoning fish and the animals that eat them. Industrial poisons also get into the soil and plants—and then are passed on to grazing animals.

Lichen takes in nutrients through air and water. If these resources are polluted, so is their food! Then, caribou and other animals that eat lichen take in the toxins, too.

The garbage left behind by some drilling companies is causing further harm to tundras.

People and the Tundra

The health of tundras is important to all of us. Soil in the top layer of permafrost is formed from the remains of plants and animals. The frozen layer locks up a huge amount of the planet's carbon. But when permafrost thaws, it releases carbon dioxide and other heat-trapping gases.

Almost half of the world's permafrost could disappear by 2100, causing temperatures to rise around the world and leading to extreme weather. Food would become harder to grow, and heat-related illnesses would increase.

Tundra permafrost also holds loose gravel, sand, and clay soil together. When too much melts, landslides become far more likely. Streams are redirected, and lakes dry up. Plants become uprooted, and animal homes are destroyed.

Tundra Life Returns

All around the world, people are realizing how important tundras are to the health of the entire planet and are finding ways to protect them.

Some countries are banning drilling and other polluting activities. At the same time, scientists are finding ways to protect tundra animal and plant life. They are also studying **endangered** tundra species such as polar bears, arctic foxes, caribou, and musk oxen, to help them survive in their changing home.

Musk oxen live in herds of 20 to 30 animals.

Some scientists suggest using herds of animals to protect tundra permafrost. The hooves of reindeer, bison, or wild horses would pack down snow, creating a thick cover that keeps permafrost cold.

Save the Tundra

Saving tundras and the life they contain seems like a huge job. But there are small, everyday steps we can take to help protect them and reduce the amount of carbon dioxide we put into the atmosphere.

If you visit the tundra, don't collect any plants or flowers. Watch any wildlife from a safe distance.

Stay on trails when walking, riding, or driving. Plants, lichen, and permafrost are easily damaged when they are trampled.

Plant trees wherever you can to help remove carbon from the atmosphere and provide food and shelter to wildlife.

Much of our electricity is made by burning fuel. Using less electricity helps the planet! Try turning down the heat and using less air conditioning. Unplug devices and chargers when they are not in use.

When it's possible and safe, ride bikes or walk instead of taking a car.

Glossary

absorbs takes in or swallows up

algae tiny plantlike living things that grow in water

atmosphere a layer of air and gases that surround Earth

bacteria tiny living things that live in water, soil, plants, and animals, and may cause illness

biodiversity the existence of many different kinds of plants and animals in an environment

biomes regions with a particular climate and environment where certain kinds of plants and animals live

carbon dioxide a gas given off when fossil fuels are burned

climate the typical weather in a place

digest to break down food into things that can be used by the body

endangered close to being killed or dying off completely

fungi plantlike things that live in or on plants, animals, or rotting material

grazing eating plant and tree materials

lichen a flat, plantlike organism made up of algae and fungi growing together

nutrients vitamins, minerals, and other substances needed by living things for health and growth

predators animals that kill and eat other animals

species groups that animals and plants are divided into according to similar characteristics

vegetation plant life

Read More

Bergin, Raymond. *Melting Ice (What on Earth? Climate Change Explained).* Minneapolis: Bearport Publishing, 2022.

Colozza Cocca, Lisa. *Tundra Animals (Biome Beasts).* North Mankato, MN: Rourke Educational Media, 2020.

Finan, Catherine C. *Plants (X-Treme Facts: Science).* Minneapolis: Bearport Publishing, 2021.

Johnson, Rebecca L. *A Walk in the Tundra (Biomes of North America), 2nd ed.* Minneapolis: Lerner Publications, 2021.

Learn More Online

1. Go to **www.factsurfer.com** or scan the QR code below.
2. Enter "**Tundra Connections**" into the search box.
3. Click on the cover of this book to see a list of websites.

Index

About the Author

Raymond Bergin lives in New Jersey, where there are forest, ocean, grassland, and wetland biomes, but—unfortunately— no tundra. Someday, he would love to visit the tundra of Baffin Island in the Canadian territory of Nunavut.